# HOW TWO CAN
# WALK TOGETHER

# HOW TWO CAN WALK TOGETHER

## A 30 DAY PRAYER AND CHALLENGE FOR CHRISTIAN COUPLES

*Gather at the Marriage Table*

*Families Made Whole Network*

BRUCE & RACHALE KELLEY

This book is intended for spiritual encouragement and educational purposes only. It is not a substitute for professional counseling, medical advice, or mental health care. If you are in a crisis or facing harm, please seek help from a qualified professional immediately.

First Edition: 2026

Printed in the United States of America

For permissions, speaking requests, or more information:

info@Familiesmadewholenetwork.com

ISBN: 978-1-7328444-1-4

Publisher/Imprint: Empowered to Be Present LLC.

# DEDICATION

This book is dedicated to every couple who has decided to walk with God through life's joy and heartaches, through healing and hope, through seasons of confusion and seasons of faith.

To marriages being strengthened, restored, and renewed.

To husbands and wives learning that unity is not found in perfection, but in a surrendered life to Christ.

May these pages remind you that love was God's idea, covenant is His design, and when He leads the way, two truly can walk together.

# INTRODUCTION

Marriage is a sacred journey designed by God to reflect His love to the world. But walking together does not happen automatically. It requires intention, humility, prayer, and a shared commitment to keep God at the center of your life.

Over the next thirty days, you and your spouse are invited to pause from the busyness of life and reconnect with God and with one another. These moments are not meant to be rushed. They are meant to be felt, prayed through, and lived out together.

Each day of this devotion will guide you to read a Scripture, reflect through a short poem, learn a simple but powerful truth, pray as one, and complete a practical couples challenge. Some days may bring encouragement and joy; others may bring conviction, healing, or honest conversation. All of it is part of the journey.

Choose a quiet time that works best for both of you - morning, afternoon, or evening (even a lunch break) when you both can be fully present. Let this be a sacred space. Let grace lead where words feel hard. Let God strengthen the bond He designed for the two of you.

As you walk through these thirty days, we pray that your love will deepen, unity will grow, and faith will be renewed. You are not walking alone. God is with you, and when He leads the way, two truly can walk together.

# HOW TO USE THIS DEVOTIONAL

This 30-day devotional was created to help couples slow down, invite God into their daily habits, and learn how to walk together in unity one step, one prayer, and one conversation at a time.

Each day is designed to be completed together; while still honoring the individual relationship each spouse has with God. You do not need a large amount of time, consistency and sincerity matter more than perfection.

## A SIMPLE DAILY RHYTHM

Each daily devotion includes:

- A Scripture to ground your hearts in God's truth

- A short poem to soften the spirit and invite reflection

- A brief lesson to foster clarity and unity

- A prayer to invite God into your marriage

- Reflection questions to encourage honest conversation

- A challenge for couples to actively demonstrate their love

# HOW TO GET THE MOST
# FROM THESE 30 DAYS

- **Commit to the journey together.** *Agree at the start to walk through all 30 days, even if you miss a day and need to return.*

- **Create a sacred space.** *Sit somewhere quiet and free from distractions. Put phones away. Let this be an intentional time.*

- **Be honest and gentle.** *Some moments may bring conviction, emotion, or discomfort. Speak truth in love and listen with grace.*

- **Pray out loud when possible.** *Even simple prayers invite God's presence and strengthen unity.*

- **Focus on progress, not perfection.** *Some days will feel powerful; others may feel quiet. God works in both.*

## IF YOU MISS A DAY

*Do not quit. Simply return where you left off. This devotional is a guide, not a rulebook. Grace is part of the process.*

## CONCLUDING REMARKS

*Marriage is not about walking perfectly; it is about walking together, with God leading every step of the way. As you commit these thirty days to prayer, reflection, and love in action, trust that God is strengthening your bond in ways you may not immediately see.*

*May this devotion become more than a book. May it become a rhythm, a reminder, and a renewed way of walking together.*

# PRAYER BEFORE YOU BEGIN

Father God,

We come before You with grateful hearts, acknowledging that our marriage is a gift from You. You are the One who joined us together, and You alone know the full purpose and calling You have placed on our union.

As we begin this 30-day journey, we invite You into every moment. Quiet the noise around us and the distractions within us. Help us to be fully present with You and with one another.

Lord, soften our hearts where they have grown guarded. Heal places where disappointment, misunderstanding, or hurt may still linger. Teach us to listen with compassion, to speak with grace, and to love as You love patiently, faithfully, and without condition.

We surrender our expectations, our pride, and our desire to be right. Replace them with humility, unity, and a shared desire to grow closer to You and to one another. Where we are strong, strengthen us more. Where we are weak, meet us with Your mercy and power.

Holy Spirit, guide our conversations. Lead our prayers. Reveal truth gently and clearly. Let these days be a turning point, not just a routine, but a renewal. May what we read, pray, and practice together take root in our hearts and transform our marriage from the inside out.

We commit this journey to You. We trust You with our past, our present, and our future. Teach us how to walk together in faith, hope, and love, hand in hand, step by step, with You leading the way.

In Jesus' name we pray, Amen.

# TABLE OF CONTENTS

# THE 30–DAY DEVOTIONAL JOURNEY

*This is where your journey begins.*

*Over the next thirty days, you will practice walking together with God one Scripture, one prayer, and one intentional step at a time. Some days will feel light and encouraging. Other days may bring honest conversations and need healing. Every day is an invitation to choose unity, grow in grace, and let love lead.*

*You don't need perfection, just presence. Show up, stay open, and let God do what only He can do in a marriage.*

*Set aside 15-25 minutes each day and complete each section together, choosing a time that allows you to be fully present with one another.*

*Let's begin.*

# DAY 1

---

## ALONE WITH GOD, STRONGER AS ONE

### SCRIPTURE FOR TODAY

*"How can two walk together unless they agree?"* (Amos 3:3)

### DAILY WALK THROUGH POEM

*When husband and wife draw near to the Lord,*
*Their hearts unite in one accord.*
*Moments alone aren't time apart.*
*God heals and tunes each waiting heart.*
*They meet again with heaven's song;*
*Their love grows deep, secure, and strong.*
*So cherish silence, seek His face;*
*You'll find each other in His grace.*

### TEACHING AND REFLECTION FOR TODAY

True unity starts with time alone in God's presence. When each spouse listens to His voice individually, they return refreshed and ready to love. Shared intimacy with the Lord keeps marriage anchored and in agreement.

## DAILY REFLECTION QUESTIONS

1. How can private prayer time make our together time stronger?

   _____

2. What can I share with my spouse from my alone time with God today?

   _____

### PRAYER FOR TODAY

Lord, teach us to value quiet moments with You. Strengthen our bond when we return to one another filled with Your peace. In Jesus' name we pray, Amen.

### DAILY COUPLE'S CHALLENGE

Spend fifteen minutes apart with God, then meet to share one thing He spoke to you.

# DAY 2

## BE A ROCK RETRIEVER, NOT A SLINGER

### SCRIPTURE FOR TODAY

*"Do not let any unwholesome word come out of your mouth..."* (Ephesians 4:29)

### DAILY WALK THROUGH POEM

*Some couples sling stones when anger's near,*
*But love retrieves the Rock of cheer.*
*Gossip and blame can tear apart,*
*Yet grace restores the wounded heart.*
*When tempers rise and words take aim,*
*Remember, love bears no one shame.*
*So reach for peace, let mercy walk;*
*Build your home through gentle talk.*

### TEACHING AND REFLECTION FOR TODAY

Words can either wound or restore. Choosing kindness over criticism protects the marriage covenant. Lean on Christ, the true Rock, and speak life over each other daily.

## DAILY REFLECTION QUESTIONS

1. What words lately have hurt or healed our connection?

_____

2. How can we practice gentler communication this week?

_____

### PRAYER FOR TODAY

*Father, guard our tongues. Let our words build, never break. Teach us to speak truth in love and reflect Your grace in our home. In Jesus' name we pray, Amen.*

### DAILY COUPLE'S CHALLENGE

*Speak one sincere compliment to your spouse today and thank God aloud for them.*

# DAY 3

⊶ ━━━⊰⊱━━━ ⊷

# PRAY TOGETHER, STRONGER FOREVER

## SCRIPTURE FOR TODAY

"For where two or three gather in My name, there am I with them."
(Matthew 18:20)

## DAILY WALK THROUGH POEM

When husband and wife join hands to pray,
Heaven leans close and lights their way.
Their voices blend, their hearts agree,
Inviting God's authority.
No mountain stands when love's combined;
Prayer unites both heart and mind.
Through storm or calm, through loss or gain,
Together they call, and God sustains.

## TEACHING AND REFLECTION FOR TODAY

Prayer is the lifeline of a thriving marriage. When couples bring every need before God as one, they find unity, protection, and renewed affection. Shared prayer draws heaven's power into the home.

## DAILY REFLECTION QUESTIONS

1. What keeps us from praying together consistently?

_____

2. Which area of our marriage most needs united prayer?

_____

### PRAYER FOR TODAY

Lord, make us a praying couple. Let Your presence dwell between us as we seek You together. In Jesus' name we pray, Amen.

### DAILY COUPLE'S CHALLENGE

Hold hands and pray out loud for each other's needs tonight.

# DAY 4

---

# BE A VOICE, CHOOSE GOD'S CHOICE

## SCRIPTURE FOR TODAY

*"Be fruitful and multiply, and fill the earth..." (Genesis 1:28)*

## DAILY WALK THROUGH POEM

*A husband's words can lift or bruise,*
*A wife's soft tone can heal or fuse.*
*Together they are God's heart and hands,*
*To bless, to teach, His truth still stands.*
*Don't hide His call or mute His grace;*
*Let love speak in every place.*
*When faith-filled voices share His care,*
*God's goodness spreads from pair to pair.*

## TEACHING AND REFLECTION FOR TODAY

God uses marriages as living testimonies. When spouses speak encouragement and share their faith openly, they become a voice of hope to others. Unity in message reveals His heart to the world.

## DAILY REFLECTION QUESTIONS

1. How does our speech reflect Christ's love?

_____

2. Who around us needs to hear hope from our story?

_____

### PRAYER FOR TODAY

Lord, use our marriage as Your instrument. Fill our mouths with kindness and our lives with witness. In Jesus' name we pray, Amen.

### DAILY COUPLE'S CHALLENGE

Share one encouraging Scripture with another couple today.

# DAY 5

## THE NARROW WAY BRINGS LIFE EACH DAY

### SCRIPTURE FOR TODAY

"Enter through the narrow gate... For the gate is small and the way is narrow that leads to life." (Matthew 7:13–14)

### DAILY WALK THROUGH POEM

As husband and wife, we choose our way;
Many roads sparkle, but few will stay.
Some promise ease, some glitter bright,
Yet only one leads to lasting light.
The narrow path may seem so small,
But walking close, we will not fall.
With Jesus first and hearts aligned,
His peace will guard both yours and mine.

### TEACHING AND REFLECTION FOR TODAY

The narrow way represents daily obedience to Christ. When couples walk this path together, they avoid distractions and grow in lasting joy. Unity comes from shared surrender to God's direction.

## DAILY REFLECTION QUESTIONS

1.  What distractions pull our focus from God's path?

   _____

2.  How can we encourage each other to stay faithful?

   _____

### PRAYER FOR TODAY

Lord, keep us steady on Your narrow way. Guard our hearts from worldly detours and make our steps one in You. In Jesus' name we pray, Amen.

### DAILY COUPLE'S CHALLENGE

Take a short walk together today and talk about one area where God is calling you to obedience.

# DAY 6

## BE THANKFUL, BE FAITHFUL

### SCRIPTURE FOR TODAY

*"Give thanks in all circumstances; for this is God's will for you in Christ Jesus." (1 Thessalonians 5:18)*

### DAILY WALK THROUGH POEM

*Be thankful for what God has done;*
*Gratitude joins two hearts as one.*
*Praise in the trial, sing through the test;*
*Faithful love blooms where thanks is blessed.*

### TEACHING AND REFLECTION FOR TODAY

*Gratitude disarms disconnection. When spouses thank God and each other daily, joy multiplies. Focus on blessings instead of flaws, and you will see your marriage prosper and thrive.*

## DAILY REFLECTION QUESTIONS

1.  What's one trait in your spouse you're grateful for today?

    _____

2.  How does gratitude change the tone of your home?

    _____

### PRAYER FOR TODAY

Father, give us thankful hearts. Teach us to notice Your gifts and to appreciate one another. In Jesus' name we pray, Amen.

### DAILY COUPLE'S CHALLENGE

Start a joint gratitude list. Each night this week, write one thing you thank God for in your spouse.

# DAY 7

## LET YOUR LIGHT SHINE TOGETHER

### SCRIPTURE FOR TODAY

"Let your light shine before others, that they may see your good deeds and glorify your Father in heaven." (Matthew 5:16)

### DAILY WALK THROUGH POEM

Through storm and calm His mercy flows;
The world sees Christ when marriage glows.
Two lights combined will brightly burn,
A beacon calling hearts to turn.

### TEACHING AND REFLECTION FOR TODAY

A unified couple reflects God's glory. Every act of forgiveness, service, or kindness becomes light for others. When your marriage radiates grace, you guide weary hearts toward Him.

## DAILY REFLECTION QUESTIONS

1.  Where can your marriage shine brighter for others this week?

    _____

2.  How can you model God's love to those who doubt it?

    _____

### PRAYER FOR TODAY

Lord, make our home a lamp of Your love. Let every action point to Your faithfulness. In Jesus' name we pray, Amen.

### DAILY COUPLE'S CHALLENGE

Do one visible act of service together, one simple kindness that reflects Christ's heart in public.

# WEEK ONE PRAYER
# STRENGTHENING OUR FOUNDATION

Lord, thank You for walking with us through these first seven days. Thank You for the awareness You've brought, the conversations You've stirred, and the unity You are building between us.

Where we have learned, help us apply.

Where we have struggled, meet us with grace.

Where You have spoken, help us obey.

Strengthen the foundation of our marriage. Teach us to seek You first, to speak life, and to choose love daily. As we move forward, keep our hearts open and our steps aligned with Your will.

In Jesus' name, Amen.

# DAY 8

## THINK HIGHER, SPEAK LIFE

### SCRIPTURE FOR TODAY

*"Be transformed by the renewing of your mind."* (Romans 12:2)

### DAILY WALK THROUGH POEM

*Keep your thoughts pure, your words aligned;*
*Lay down what's heavy, renew the mind.*
*Faith builds bridges; fear pulls down.*
*Choose words that heal, not words that drown.*

### TEACHING AND REFLECTION FOR TODAY

The tone you set with your thoughts shapes your union. When you both reject negativity and speak faith, you invite peace into your home. Think higher, speak life, and hope will stay alive between you.

## DAILY REFLECTION QUESTIONS

1. What words most often discourage your spouse?

_____

2. What uplifting truth could you speak instead?

_____

### PRAYER FOR TODAY

Lord, cleanse our thoughts and steady our speech. Let encouragement fill every corner of our marriage. In Jesus' name we pray, Amen.

### DAILY COUPLE'S CHALLENGE

For the next 24 hours, replace every complaint with gratitude and one spoken word of praise.

# DAY 9

## SERVE WHOLEHEARTEDLY, TOGETHER

### SCRIPTURE FOR TODAY

*"Whatever you do, do your work heartily, as for the Lord and not for men."*
(Colossians 3:23)

### DAILY WALK THROUGH POEM

*Offer your time, your love, your all;*
*Answer with joy when duty calls.*
*Serve together with hearts that sing.*
*God blesses every faithful and thoughtful thing.*

### TEACHING AND REFLECTION FOR TODAY

When couples give God excellence rather than leftovers, they experience abundance. Your shared service, whether in ministry or daily life, invites His presence to dwell richly in your home.

## DAILY REFLECTION QUESTIONS

1. Where might you be giving God "what's left" instead of your best?

_____

2. How can serving together strengthen your bond?

_____

### PRAYER FOR TODAY

Lord, help us offer You our first and finest. Let our teamwork bring You glory.

In Jesus' name we pray, Amen.

### DAILY COUPLE'S CHALLENGE

Choose one task this week to complete together as an offering to God.

# DAY 10

---

# FAITH THAT HOLDS YOU STEADY

## SCRIPTURE FOR TODAY

> "If you have faith as small as a mustard seed ... nothing will be impossible for you." (Matthew 17:20)

## DAILY WALK THROUGH POEM

Faith is the anchor when tempests roar.
It steadies the heart forevermore.
Though waves may rise and fear may shout,
Faith pulls weary sailors out.

## TEACHING AND REFLECTION FOR TODAY

Faith unites when sight confuses. When storms test your love, cling to what God promised, not what you feel. Shared faith transforms panic into peace and draws you close again.

## DAILY REFLECTION QUESTIONS

1. Where do you need to believe in God together today?

_____

2. How has faith strengthened your relationship in past trials?

_____

## PRAYER FOR TODAY

_Lord, increase our faith beyond what we see. Let trust be our anchor through every storm. In Jesus' name we pray, Amen._

## DAILY COUPLE'S CHALLENGE

_When a worry arises, stop and pray together before discussing it. Let faith lead every decision._

# DAY 11

## STAY FOCUSED ON THE ROAD AHEAD

### SCRIPTURE FOR TODAY

*"Let your eyes look straight ahead; fix your gaze directly before you."* (Proverbs 4:25)

### DAILY WALK THROUGH POEM

Crossroads come to test your sight,
Keep walking forward in God's light.
Distractions whisper, "Turn aside,"
But peace will come when hearts abide.
One purpose, one vision, side by side,
Through every turn, let God be your guide.
His Word will lead, His promises true,
He clears the path prepared for you.

### TEACHING AND REFLECTION FOR TODAY

Distractions can divide a marriage. Stay focused on where God is leading you together. When you pray before deciding, His peace will confirm your steps. Trust His direction, not your emotions or outside pressures.

## DAILY REFLECTION QUESTIONS

1. What distractions have pulled your marriage off course lately?

   _____

2. How can you help one another stay focused on what truly matters?

   _____

### PRAYER FOR TODAY

Lord, align our hearts with Yours. Keep our focus steady on Your path of purpose and peace. In Jesus' name we pray, Amen.

### DAILY COUPLE'S CHALLENGE

This week, choose one shared goal to pursue together and pray over it daily.

# DAY 12

---

## STAND FIRM LIKE A TREE

### SCRIPTURE FOR TODAY

*"He will be like a tree planted by streams of water, which yields its fruit in season."* (Psalm 1:3)

### DAILY WALK THROUGH POEM

When winds arise and branches sway,
Roots in Christ will never give way.
Storms may rage, the sky may frown,
But trees of faith will not fall down.
Stand together, firm and strong,
Your roots in love will last lifelong.
God waters hearts that don't let go,
And steady love continues to grow.

### TEACHING AND REFLECTION FOR TODAY

Every marriage faces seasons of testing. Strength doesn't come from avoiding storms, but from being rooted in God's Word. The deeper your roots, the greater your fruit. Hold fast together when pressure comes.

## DAILY REFLECTION QUESTIONS

1. What trials have strengthened your marriage roots?

   _____

2. How can you better "water" your relationship with prayer and patience?

   _____

### PRAYER FOR TODAY

Lord, plant us deep in Your truth. Help our love remain steadfast through every storm. In Jesus' name we pray, Amen.

### DAILY COUPLE'S CHALLENGE

Read Psalm 1 together and discuss what "bearing fruit" means for your marriage in this season.

# DAY 13

---

# RETURN TO YOUR FIRST LOVE

## SCRIPTURE FOR TODAY

*"Yet I hold this against you: You have forsaken the love you had at first."* (Revelation 2:4)

## DAILY WALK THROUGH POEM

*Remember love's beginning flame,*
*When joy was fresh and hearts the same.*
*The years may dim what once was bright,*
*But renewed love restores the light.*
*Return to laughter, prayer, and grace;*
*Invite His presence to that space.*
*The God who joined your hearts above*
*Still whispers, "Come back to your first love."*

## TEACHING AND REFLECTION FOR TODAY

Sometimes routine replaces romance and duty overshadows devotion. God invites couples to rekindle their passion for Him and for each other. Choose to remember, to laugh, and to cherish again.

## DAILY REFLECTION QUESTIONS

1. What first-love moments do you miss and want to revive?

   _____

2. How can you show affection or kindness in a new way this week?

   _____

### PRAYER FOR TODAY

Lord, restore our tenderness and joy. Remind us why You joined our hearts together.

In Jesus' name we pray, Amen.

### DAILY COUPLE'S CHALLENGE

Plan one simple "first love" activity together, a walk, a song, or a meal that brings back gratitude and joy.

# DAY 14

---

# LET IT RAIN AND GROW AGAIN

## SCRIPTURE FOR TODAY

*"I have set my rainbow in the clouds, and it will be the sign of the covenant."*
(Genesis 9:13)

## DAILY WALK THROUGH POEM

Rain may fall and skies may cry,
But growth begins when hearts rely.
Through storm and flood His grace remains,
And faith revives what pain constrains.
After the rain, His promise stands,
A rainbow stretched by loving hands.
What seemed to end was made anew,
For God keeps covenant with you.

## TEACHING AND REFLECTION FOR TODAY

Hard times are often God's way of watering seeds we didn't know were planted. Don't resent the rain. Let it cleanse, soften, and prepare your hearts for new growth.

## Daily Reflection Questions

1. How has a past trial brought new growth in your relationship?

_____

2. What promise are you trusting God to fulfill right now?

_____

## PRAYER FOR TODAY

Lord, help us see Your purpose in every storm. Let Your promise shine brighter than our pain. In Jesus' name we pray, Amen.

## DAILY COUPLE'S CHALLENGE

During your next disagreement, pause and pray before reacting. Let God bring peace through the rain.

# WEEK TWO PRAYER
# GROWING THROUGH THE STORMS

*Father God, thank You for Your faithfulness through every season. Thank You for reminding us that rain produces growth and that storms do not destroy what You have planted.*

*Help us trust You when the path feels narrow or unclear. Teach us to walk in obedience, gratitude, and perseverance. Let what we have faced together deepen our faith rather than divide our hearts.*

*We choose to believe that You are working all things together for our good and Your glory. Strengthen our unity, renew our hope, and prepare our hearts for what lies ahead.*

*In Jesus' name, Amen.*

# DAY 15

---

# WHAT GOD HAS FOR YOU IS YOURS

## SCRIPTURE FOR TODAY

*"No weapon formed against you will prosper."* (Isaiah 54:17)

## DAILY WALK THROUGH POEM

No one can take what God has sealed.
His promises are firm and real.
Though storms may rise and doubts may start,
What He has given guards your heart.

## TEACHING AND REFLECTION FOR TODAY

Comparison poisons contentment. God's gifts are specific to you and your marriage. When you focus on your calling rather than another's, peace returns. Trust in His timing and His plan.

## DAILY REFLECTION QUESTIONS

1.  In what areas are you tempted to compare your marriage to others?

    _____

2.  How can you celebrate what God is doing in your spouse's life?

    _____

### PRAYER FOR TODAY

*Lord, silence every voice that breeds doubt or envy. Help us stay confident in Your promises for our family. In Jesus' name we pray, Amen.*

### DAILY COUPLE'S CHALLENGE

*Each morning this week, declare aloud: "What God has for us is ours." Watch how it changes your confidence and gratitude.*

# DAY 16

## GUARD YOUR PEACE

### SCRIPTURE FOR TODAY

*"And the peace of God, which transcends all understanding, will guard your hearts and your minds in Christ Jesus." (Philippians 4:7)*

### DAILY WALK THROUGH POEM

*Guard your peace, protect your space,*
*Let love abide, and set the pace.*
*When voices rise and tempers flare,*
*Remember grace, for God is there.*
*Peace is power, soft but strong,*
*It rights the heart when things go wrong.*
*When marriage rests in a calm embrace,*
*The Lord Himself fills every place.*

### TEACHING AND REFLECTION FOR TODAY

Peace doesn't mean the absence of problems; it's the presence of God in the middle of them. When tension enters your home, invite Him first. Guarding your peace protects your connection.

## DAILY REFLECTION QUESTIONS

1.  What usually steals your peace as a couple?

_____

2.  How can you guard your hearts before conflict escalates?

_____

### PRAYER FOR TODAY

Lord, fill our home with Your peace. Help us choose calm words and patient hearts.

In Jesus' name we pray, Amen.

### DAILY COUPLE'S CHALLENGE

When stress rises today, pause for ten seconds of silent prayer before speaking.

# DAY 17

<hr/>

# BUILD ON SOLID GROUND

## SCRIPTURE FOR TODAY

*"For no one can lay any foundation other than the one already laid, which is Jesus Christ." (1 Corinthians 3:11)*

## DAILY WALK THROUGH POEM

Build your home on truth, not sand,
Hold together hand in hand.
Storms may test what love has grown,
But Christ will keep what is His own.
If walls should shake and doubts abound,
Return again to solid ground.
The Rock of Ages will not fall,
He guards the hearts that give Him all.

## TEACHING AND REFLECTION FOR TODAY

Every decision, dream, and plan in marriage must rest on Christ. When you build on feelings, things shift; when you build on faith, they stand. Keep returning to the foundation of prayer and Scripture.

## DAILY REFLECTION QUESTIONS

1.  What part of your marriage most needs to be rebuilt on Christ?

    _____

2.  How can prayer reinforce your foundation this week?

    _____

### PRAYER FOR TODAY

Lord, strengthen the structure of our love. Let every part of our home be built on You.

In Jesus' name we pray, Amen.

### DAILY COUPLE'S CHALLENGE

Write one "foundation verse" on paper and place it somewhere visible in your home.

# DAY 18

## FORGIVE QUICKLY, LOVE DEEPLY

### SCRIPTURE FOR TODAY

*"Bear with each other and forgive one another if any of you has a grievance against someone. Forgive as the Lord forgave you." (Colossians 3:13)*

### DAILY WALK THROUGH POEM

*Forgive the words that cut too deep,*
*Release the pain you cannot keep.*
*Mercy heals where pride once stood,*
*Let love do what only it could.*
*Quick to pardon, slow to blame,*
*Grace restores and ends the shame.*
*When hearts forgive, God's joy will stay,*
*And peace will crown the hurt away.*

### TEACHING AND REFLECTION FOR TODAY

Unforgiveness locks two hearts in separate rooms. When you choose mercy, you unlock freedom. Forgiveness doesn't excuse wrong; it invites healing.

## DAILY REFLECTION QUESTIONS

1.  What hurt do you still need to release to your spouse or to God?

    _____

2.  How does forgiveness strengthen your unity?

    _____

### PRAYER FOR TODAY

*Lord, help us forgive as You forgive us. Heal the memories that still ache.*

*In Jesus' name we pray, Amen.*

### DAILY COUPLE'S CHALLENGE

*Speak these words aloud together: "I choose to forgive and to be free."*

# DAY 19

---

## SPEAK TRUTH IN LOVE

### SCRIPTURE FOR TODAY

*"Instead, speaking the truth in love, we will grow to become in every respect the mature body of Him who is the head, that is, Christ." (Ephesians 4:15)*

### DAILY WALK THROUGH POEM

*Truth without love can break apart,*
*But love with lies will wound the heart.*
*Together speak what must be said,*
*With gentle tone and prayer instead.*
*Words can build or words can bruise,*
*So let your lips, the Spirit, use.*
*When honesty and grace agree,*
*The home reflects His purity.*

### TEACHING AND REFLECTION FOR TODAY

*Healthy marriages thrive on honesty. Speak truth kindly, listen humbly, and let correction draw you closer instead of apart. God's love never hides from truth.*

## DAILY REFLECTION QUESTIONS

1. Do you find it harder to be honest or to be gentle?

_____

2. How can you both create safety for truthful conversation?

_____

### PRAYER FOR TODAY

Lord, teach us to speak truth with compassion. Let honesty be our habit and love our motive. In Jesus' name we pray, Amen.

### DAILY COUPLE'S CHALLENGE

Have one short "heart talk" today where you each share a truth in love, then pray afterward.

# DAY 20

## REST AND RESTORE

### Scripture for Today

> "Come to me, all you who are weary and burdened, and I will give you rest."
> (Matthew 11:28)

### Daily Walk Through Poem

Rest your hearts, release the strain,
Let His presence soothe the pain.
Work will wait, but love must mend,
Find stillness where His mercies blend.
In quiet peace the soul can heal,
God renews what stress can steal.
When two slow down at Heaven's door,
They rise refreshed to love once more.

### Teaching and Reflection for Today

Rest is holy. Busyness without balance wears love thin. God calls couples to slow down together to laugh, to breathe, to remember why they said "I do."

## DAILY REFLECTION QUESTIONS

1. What rhythms of rest refresh your marriage most?

_____

2. How can you protect Sabbath-style peace in your home?

_____

### PRAYER FOR TODAY

Lord, teach us to rest in You and with each other. Restore our joy and renew our strength. In Jesus' name we pray, Amen.

### DAILY COUPLE'S CHALLENGE

Schedule one "no-task" evening this week, phones down, hearts up, just time together.

# DAY 21

---

## SERVE ONE ANOTHER IN LOVE

### SCRIPTURE FOR TODAY

*"Serve one another humbly in love."* (Galatians 5:13)

### DAILY WALK THROUGH POEM

*Love is strongest when hands obey,*
*Serving each other day by day.*
*Small acts of care, a gentle tone,*
*Turn house and heart to a sacred home.*
*When one gives joy and one receives,*
*Heaven smiles and never leaves.*
*The more you serve, the more you find,*
*Two hearts made one in Christ's design.*

### TEACHING AND REFLECTION FOR TODAY

Service is love in motion. When you put your spouse's needs before your own, pride dies and unity grows. Marriage thrives on humility and daily acts of care.

## DAILY REFLECTION QUESTIONS

1. How does your spouse feel most loved by your actions?

   _____

2. What small act of service could bless them today?

   _____

### PRAYER FOR TODAY

*Lord, teach us to serve with glad hearts. Let our love be known through kindness and deeds, not only words. In Jesus' name we pray, Amen.*

### DAILY COUPLE'S CHALLENGE

*Do one task for your spouse today without being asked, simply as worship to God.*

# WEEK THREE PRAYER
# GUARDING UNITY AND PEACE

Lord, thank You for the work You are doing in our hearts and in our marriage. Thank You for teaching us how to love through forgiveness, honesty, rest, and service.

We ask You now to guard the unity You have been building. Protect our peace from distractions, misunderstandings, and outside pressures. Help us to listen before reacting, to forgive quickly, and to choose humility over pride.

When tension tries to enter our home, remind us to pause and invite You in first. Let Your peace rules our hearts, Your wisdom guide our words, and Your love shape our actions.

Bind us together with patience, compassion, and understanding as we continue walking forward side by side. May our marriage reflect Your heart and bring You glory.

In Jesus' name, Amen.

# DAY 22

<hr/>

## BE QUICK TO LISTEN

### SCRIPTURE FOR TODAY

*"Everyone should be quick to listen, slow to speak and slow to become angry."* (James 1:19)

### DAILY WALK THROUGH POEM

*Listen first, then choose your reply,*
*Soft words calm while harsh ones fly.*
*Ears that hear with love and grace*
*Keep peace alive in every place.*
*Silence often speaks more true*
*Then all the words we rush into.*
*When hearts feel heard, they rest again,*
*And healing flows where hurt had been.*

### TEACHING AND REFLECTION FOR TODAY

Listening is one of the purest forms of love. Arguments fade when understanding grows. Make space to truly hear, not just respond, and your marriage will breathe easier.

## DAILY REFLECTION QUESTIONS

1.  What keeps you from listening with full attention?

_____

2.  How can you remind each other to slow down before replying?

_____

### PRAYER FOR TODAY

Lord, quiet our minds so we can listen well. Let understanding guard our home.

In Jesus' name we pray, Amen.

### DAILY COUPLE'S CHALLENGE

For one conversation today, focus only on hearing, no advice, no correction, just listening.

# DAY 23

## KEEP HOPE ALIVE

### SCRIPTURE FOR TODAY

"Let us hold unswervingly to the hope we profess, for He who promised is faithful." (Hebrews 10:23)

### DAILY WALK THROUGH POEM

When dreams seem far and prayers delayed,
Hope still whispers, "Be not afraid."
God's timing perfect, plans divine,
In waiting He refines the line.
Hold to His word when nights feel long,
Hope's gentle thread will make you strong.
Together trust the path unseen,
For faithful love stands in between.

### TEACHING AND REFLECTION FOR TODAY

Hope is the bridge between prayer and fulfillment. Couples anchored in hope don't give up when life feels slow. Keep believing God's delays are not His denials.

## Daily Reflection Questions

1. Where do you need renewed hope as a couple?

_____

2. How can you encourage your spouse while you both wait?

_____

## PRAYER FOR TODAY

_Lord, renew our hope where weariness has grown. Teach us to wait with faith and gratitude. In Jesus' name we pray, Amen._

## DAILY COUPLE'S CHALLENGE

_Speak one hopeful promise of Scripture aloud together each morning this week._

# DAY 24

# WALK IN UNITY

## SCRIPTURE FOR TODAY

"Make every effort to keep the unity of the Spirit through the bond of peace."
(Ephesians 4:3)

## DAILY WALK THROUGH POEM

Two can't walk if steps divide,
Keep stride with love, stay side by side.
Disagreements need not break apart,
When Christ's own peace rules every heart.
Unity is not the same,
Its purpose joined in Jesus' name.
Different voices, single song,
Together right where both belong.

## TEACHING AND REFLECTION FOR TODAY

Unity takes effort. You won't always think alike, but you can choose to move in the same direction. Let humility be the bridge when opinions differ.

## Daily Reflection Questions

1. What causes disunity in your relationship most often?

_____

2. How can you make peace your first priority?

_____

### PRAYER FOR TODAY

Lord, knit our hearts in harmony. Make our marriage one in spirit and in aim.

In Jesus' name we pray, Amen

### DAILY COUPLE'S CHALLENGE

Pray together before major decisions, asking God to align your hearts before your plans.

# DAY 25

## LET LOVE LEAD

### SCRIPTURE FOR TODAY

*"Do everything in love." (1 Corinthians 16:14)*

### DAILY WALK THROUGH POEM

*Let love be captain, strong yet kind,*
*Guiding the heart and steering the mind.*
*When tempers flare or patience ends,*
*Let love remind you both of friends.*
*Love is gentle, brave, and true,*
*It sees the best in all you do.*
*When love leads first, pride falls behind,*
*And heaven's peace is what you find.*

### TEACHING AND REFLECTION FOR TODAY

Love is the foundation and the compass. When conflict arises, ask, "What would love do?" That question alone can turn any moment into ministry.

## DAILY REFLECTION QUESTIONS

1. What does "letting love lead" look like in your marriage right now?

   _____

2. How can you show love first instead of waiting for your spouse to?

   _____

### PRAYER FOR TODAY

Lord, help us lead with love in every word and action. Let compassion guide how we speak and respond. In Jesus' name we pray, Amen.

### DAILY COUPLE'S CHALLENGE

Before you respond in frustration, pause and pray, "Lord, let love lead."

# DAY 26

## CHOOSE JOY DAILY

### SCRIPTURE FOR TODAY

*"The joy of the Lord is your strength."* (Nehemiah 8:10, NIV)

### DAILY WALK THROUGH POEM

*Joy is not a fleeting mood,*
*It's a strength in every attitude.*
*When laughter fades and days grow long,*
*Joy still sings a steady song.*
*Happiness shifts, but joy will stay,*
*When Christ is in the center every day.*
*Together smile through tears and test,*
*For joy in Him will give you rest.*

### TEACHING AND REFLECTION FOR TODAY

Joy is a choice, not a circumstance. A joyful heart keeps a marriage light even in heavy seasons. When both spouses choose gratitude over gloom, peace multiplies.

## DAILY REFLECTION QUESTIONS

1. What steals your joy most often?

   _____

2. How can you remind each other to look for God's goodness in small things?

   _____

### PRAYER FOR TODAY

Lord, restore the joy of our salvation. Let laughter and gratitude fill our home.

In Jesus 'name we pray, Amen.

### DAILY COUPLE'S CHALLENGE

Find one reason to laugh together today. Joy is holy medicine.

# DAY 27

## PRACTICE PATIENCE

### SCRIPTURE FOR TODAY

"Be completely humble and gentle; be patient, bearing with one another in love." (Ephesians 4:2)

### DAILY WALK THROUGH POEM

Patience waits when tempers burn,
It gives love time for hearts to turn.
No rush, no race, no angry word,
Just quiet trust in what's preferred.
Like rivers carving gentle ways,
Patience shapes the heart that prays.
When husband, wife, let grace extend,
Their waiting brings a peaceful end.

### TEACHING AND REFLECTION FOR TODAY

Impatience is love's enemy. Marriage grows best in the slow work of grace. Allow room for each other's weaknesses. Time and tenderness can fix what tension never could.

## DAILY REFLECTION QUESTIONS

1. What moments test your patience most with your spouse?

   _____

2. How can you give grace in those moments rather than react?

   _____

### PRAYER FOR TODAY

Lord, teach us to wait with compassion. Let patience fill our speech and silence alike.

In Jesus' name we pray, Amen.

### DAILY COUPLE'S CHALLENGE

Pause before responding today. Take one deep breath and ask God for calmness.

# DAY 28

---

# KEEP YOUR COVENANT STRONG

## SCRIPTURE FOR TODAY

"Therefore what God has joined together, let no one separate." (Mark 10:9)

## DAILY WALK THROUGH POEM

Vows are more than words we say,
They bind two hearts in God's own way.
Through storm or calm, through gain or loss,
Love bears the weight, it lifts the cross.
A promise held, a faith made real,
No lie or trial can break that seal.
For covenant is love's pure song,
The sacred bond that makes you strong.

## TEACHING AND REFLECTION FOR TODAY

Your marriage is a covenant, not a contract. It's held together by God's grace, not human perfection. When you remember your vow before Him, endurance rises where feelings fall.

## DAILY REFLECTION QUESTIONS

1.  What do your vows mean to you today?

 

2.  How can you honor your covenant through daily choices?

### PRAYER FOR TODAY

Lord, remind us that our union is sacred. Help us protect what You have joined.

In Jesus' name we pray, Amen.

### DAILY COUPLE'S CHALLENGE

Revisit your vows together. Read them aloud or write new ones reflecting how far God has brought you.

# DAY 29

## KEEP THE FIRE BURNING

### SCRIPTURE FOR TODAY

*"Many waters cannot quench love; rivers cannot sweep it away."* (Song of Solomon 8:7)

### DAILY WALK THROUGH POEM

*Flames of love may flicker low,*
*But embers wait beneath to glow.*
*Fan the spark with tender care,*
*Let laughter, prayer, and time repair.*
*Romance fades if left untended,*
*But passion grows when grace is blended.*
*When hearts pursue what once began,*
*They find again the warmth of God's plan.*

### TEACHING AND REFLECTION FOR TODAY

Love isn't lost; it just needs tending. Marriage thrives when you invest in connection, date nights, affection, and prayer. Keep rediscovering the one you promised to love.

## DAILY REFLECTION QUESTIONS

1.  What keeps the "fire" alive in your marriage?

    _____

2.  What could you intentionally do this week to reconnect?

    _____

### PRAYER FOR TODAY

_Lord, reignite the fire of intimacy and joy. Teach us to pursue each other with kindness and care. In Jesus' name we pray, Amen._

### DAILY COUPLE'S CHALLENGE

_Plan one intentional time of closeness this week, talk, laugh, or share a memory that rekindles warmth._

# DAY 30

---

# WALK TOGETHER IN LOVE

## SCRIPTURE FOR TODAY

*"And now these three remain: faith, hope and love. But the greatest of these is love." (1 Corinthians 13:13)*

## DAILY WALK THROUGH POEM

Faith will guide and hope will cheer,
But love remains when all draws near.
Through every test, through gain or loss,
True love looks daily to the cross.
Walk hand in hand, your journey one,
Until His work with you is done.
Let every step and breath you take
Be love for Jesus, for His sake.

## TEACHING AND REFLECTION FOR TODAY

Marriage is a lifelong walk of love. Faith gives direction, hope gives courage, and love gives endurance. Keep choosing to love every day, it's the key that unlocks joy until eternity.

## Daily Reflection Questions

1. What has God taught you through this 30-day journey?

   _____

2. How will you continue strengthening your faith, hope, and love together?

   _____

### PRAYER FOR TODAY

Lord, thank You for guiding us these thirty days. May we walk together in love for all our days ahead. In Jesus' name we pray, Amen.

### DAILY COUPLE'S CHALLENGE

Renew your commitment to walk hand in hand with God and one another. Write down your next goal as a couple and pray over it.

# WEEK FOUR PRAYER
# WALKING FORWARD IN LOVE

Father God,

Thank You for walking with us through these thirty days. Thank You for the conversations we've had, the prayers we've prayed, and the growth You've begun in our hearts and in our marriage.

As we move forward, help us carry these lessons into everyday life. Teach us to keep choosing love when it would be easier to withdraw, to keep listening when emotions run high, and to keep forgiving as You have forgiven us.

Strengthen our covenant. Guard our unity. Let faith guide our decisions, hope anchor our future, and love leads our words and actions. When challenges arise, remind us that we are not walking alone, You are with us, and we are with each other.

We commit our marriage, our family and our future to You. Teach us to keep walking together, hand in hand, heart to heart, with You at the center.

In Jesus' name, Amen.

# AFTERWORD
# KEEP WALKING TOGETHER

You've reached the end of this 30-day journey, but not the end of your walk. What you've done here matters. Every prayer, every conversation, every moment of intentional love has planted seeds that God will continue to grow.

Marriage is not sustained by perfection, but by perseverance. It's built in daily choices to listen, to forgive, to serve, and to keep God at the center. Some seasons will feel light and joyful; others will stretch your faith. In all of them, God remains faithful.

As you move forward, keep choosing to walk together. Return to prayer when words feel hard. Return to Scripture when direction feels unclear. Return to love when life feels heavy.

May your marriage continue to be strengthened by faith, anchored in hope, and led by love.

Keep walking together.

# AUTHOR'S NOTE

This devotional was written from a place of prayer, experience, and deep love for marriage as God designed it to be.

For over three decades, we have walked through the beauty and the challenges of marriage, through seasons of joy, growth, stretching, and refinement. Along the way, God has continually reminded us that marriage is not sustained by feelings alone, but by faith, commitment, humility, and His presence at the center.

These pages were created to offer couples a simple, intentional way to pause, pray, and reconnect with God and with one another. Nothing here is meant to be rushed or perfected. It is meant to be lived out, one day at a time, with grace.

If this devotional has encouraged you, challenged you, or helped you see your marriage with fresh eyes, we thank God for that. Our prayer is that what you've begun here continues long after these pages end, that prayer remains a rhythm, communication stays tender, and love keeps leading your home.

Thank you for allowing us to walk alongside you for these thirty days. It is an honor to share this journey with you.

With love and prayers,

**Bruce & Rachale Kelley**

Families Made Whole Network

# ACKNOWLEDGMENT

*First and foremost, we give all honor and glory to our Lord and Savior, Jesus Christ. Without His grace, wisdom, and faithfulness, this work would not exist. Every truth shared in these pages flows from His Word and His unfailing love.*

*We are deeply grateful for the pastors, leaders, mentors, and prayer partners who have poured into our lives and marriage over the years. Your guidance, encouragement, and example have strengthened us and shaped the ministry God has entrusted to us.*

To the couples who have allowed us to walk alongside them—thank you for your honesty, trust, and willingness to grow. Your stories, struggles, and victories have continually reminded us that love rooted in Christ truly heals.

We also extend heartfelt thanks to our family for your patience, prayers, and unwavering support. Your love has been a constant source of strength.

Above all, we acknowledge God's hand in every step of this journey. May this devotion bring Him glory and bless every marriage that opens its pages

# ABOUT THE AUTHORS

Bruce and Rachale Kelley are the founders of Families Made Whole Network, a faith-based marriage and family ministry dedicated to uniting couples, strengthening families, and building legacies rooted in God's design. Married for 33 years, they believe healthy, aligned marriages create stability, love, and direction for the whole family.

For more than three decades, Bruce Kelley has served as a counselor, coach, and minister, guiding husbands, couples, and families into healing and wholeness. He holds a bachelor's degree from Bowling Green State University and a Master of Divinity from Winebrenner Theological Seminary. He is the author of 90 Days with God and co-author of the best-selling What the Preacher Didn't Say at the Altar.

Rachale Kelley is a passionate teacher, mentor, and ministry leader with a heart for restoration and generational healing. A devoted wife and former stay-at-home mom, she brings a compassionate, family-centered perspective to help couples rebuild emotional safety and restore unity. They are parents of three children, including a son with Down syndrome and autism, and their family journey has strengthened their commitment to helping homes thrive. Together, they create safe, faith-filled spaces where relationships don't just survive, they heal, thrive, and leave a legacy.

Connect on Facebook: Gather at the Marriage Table
https://www.facebook.com/gatheratthetabe

# PERSONAL NOTES

# Thank you for reading
# this 30-Day Marriage Devotional!

*If you have enjoyed this book and found it helpful in your marriage, kindly leave a review on the Amazon listing. This small gesture helps in a BIG way in spreading the Word of God.*
*Amen.*

*Follow Bruce and Rachale Kelley on their*

*Amazon Author Central Pageor reach them at*

*info@Familiesmadewholenetwork.com*